DIFFERENT WAYS TO RECEIVE HEALING FROM SCRIPTURE AND WALK IN HEALTH

Bisi Oladipupo

Springs of life publishing

CONTENTS

Title Page

Copyright

Dedication 1

Foreword 2

A Word for Someone 4

Chapter 1 6

Chapter 2 8

Chapter 3 10

Chapter 4 12

Chapter 5 14

Chapter 6 15

Chapter 7 17

Chapter 8 18

Chapter 9 20

Chapter 10 22

Chapter 11 24

Chapter 12 26

Chapter 13   28

Chapter 14   30

Chapter 15   31

Chapter 16   36

Chapter 17   37

Chapter 18   38

Chapter 19   39

Conclusion   41

Salvation Prayer   43

About The Author   44

Other Books by Bisi   45

DEDICATION

To Jesus Christ, my Lord and Saviour—to Him alone that laid down His life that l might have life eternal. To Him that led captivity captive and gave gifts unto men (Ephesians 4:8). One of those gifts is writing!

FOREWORD

Scripture makes it very clear that healing belongs to us.

Here are just a few scriptures to confirm this:

*"Beloved, I wish above all things that thou mayest prosper and **be in health**, even as thy soul prospereth"* (3 John 2).

"Who his own self bare our sins in his own body on the tree, that we, being dead to sins, should live unto righteousness: by whose stripes ye were healed" (1 Peter 2:24).

So, it is clear from Scripture that healing belongs to us, as Jesus Christ has already borne all our sicknesses.

When it comes to the salvation that makes Jesus Christ the Lord and Saviour of our lives, many people effortlessly understand this.

Once again, Scripture makes it explicit what sinner needs to do to come to Christ Jesus.

"That if thou shalt confess with thy mouth the Lord Jesus, and shalt believe in thine heart that God hath raised him from the dead, thou shalt be saved. For with the heart man believeth unto righteousness; and with

the mouth confession is made unto salvation" (Romans 10:9-10).

"*For whosoever shall call upon the name of the Lord shall be saved*" (Romans 10:13).

Many of us have heard a wide variety of testimonies of how people came to know the Lord. Some just called upon the Lord in their living rooms; some came out and responded to an altar call, while others just cried out to the Lord from wherever they were. The response from the Lord is the same.

"*All that the Father giveth me shall come to me; and him that cometh to me I will in no wise cast out*" (John 6:37).

When it comes to healing, different camps have different approaches of how to receive healing.

This book will look at the different ways healing can be received from Scripture and touch on some biblical principles to walk in health.

Bisi Oladipupo

A WORD FOR SOMEONE

When you look through Scripture, there are accounts of many healings, both in the Old and New Testaments.

Did you notice that most healings did not occur the same way? The woman with the issue of blood touched His garment and was healed (Matthew 9:20–22). Jesus anointed a blind man's eyes with clay and told him to wash it off in the pool of Siloam. He acted on the instruction and was healed (John 9:1-7). Peter spoke to the lame man at the gate and ordered him to get up in Jesus' name, and he was healed (Acts 3:1-8). All these are just a few of many accounts of healing from the Scripture.

Also, many principles in Scripture can be applied to receiving healing today. Everyone's healing journey is different; therefore, don't compare yourself with others.

Ultimately, the Holy Spirit will guide us into all truth. The Lord knows where we are at and what truth He needs to bring across our paths.

One thing is sure, if God did not withhold Jesus Christ from us but freely gave Him up for us all

(Romans 8:32), rest assured that He is not withholding any good thing from us.

Let us now examine the diverse ways people received healing from the Bible. We will also examine scriptural principles that can be applied to receive healing and walk in health.

Some of the examples of healing may be repeated in different sections of the book. This is because several principles can be learnt from the same healing.

Be encouraged!

CHAPTER 1

By Speaking to The Situation

From Scripture, speaking to the situation and commanding healing is one way some people do receive healing.

Let us look at a few examples from Scripture:

"And, behold, there was a man which had his hand withered. And they asked him, saying, Is it lawful to heal on the sabbath days? that they might accuse him. And he said unto them, What man shall there be among you, that shall have one sheep, and if it fall into a pit on the sabbath day, will he not lay hold on it, and lift it out? How much then is a man better than a sheep? Wherefore it is lawful to do well on the sabbath days. **Then saith he to the man, Stretch forth thine hand**. *And he stretched it forth; and it was restored whole, like as the other"* (Matthew 12:10-13).

Here, you can see that our Lord Jesus Christ just told the man to stretch forth his hand, and the man's hand was restored.

"And he arose out of the synagogue, and entered into Simon's house. And Simon's wife's mother was taken with a great fever; and they besought him for her. And he stood over her, and **rebuked the fever***; and it left her: and immediately she arose and ministered unto them"* (Luke 4:38-39).

We can see from this scripture that our Lord Jesus Christ rebuked the fever, and it left.

Both the man in the Book of Matthew and Simon Peter's mother-in-law received their healing by the Lord speaking to their situation.

"*For verily I say unto you, That whosoever shall say unto this mountain, Be thou removed, and be thou cast into the sea; and shall not doubt in his heart, but shall believe that those things which he saith shall come to pass; he shall have whatsoever he saith*" (Mark 11:23).

"***Death and life are in the power of the tongue****: and they that love it shall eat the fruit thereof*" (Proverbs 18:21).

CHAPTER 2

By Acknowledging What
We Have in Christ

What we have been given in Christ are spiritual realities that need to become real to us.

Peter gave the man at the beautiful gate what he had, and the lame man was healed.

"Now Peter and John went up together into the temple at the hour of prayer, being the ninth hour. [2] And a certain man lame from his mother's womb was carried, whom they laid daily at the gate of the temple which is called Beautiful, to ask alms of them that entered into the temple; [3] Who seeing Peter and John about to go into the temple asked an alms. [4] And Peter, fastening his eyes upon him with John, said, Look on us. [5] And he gave heed unto them, expecting to receive something of them. [6] Then Peter said, Silver and gold have I none; **but such as I have give I thee: In the name of Jesus** *Christ of Nazareth rise up and walk. [7] And he took him by the right hand, and lifted him up: and immediately his feet and ankle bones received strength. [8] And he leaping*

up stood, and walked, and entered with them into the temple, walking, and leaping, and praising God. ⁹ And all the people saw him walking and praising God" (Acts 3:1-9).

This is one account where we see a disciple say, "Such as l have give l thee".

The good news is that as believers, we all have been given the name of Jesus Christ.

"That the communication of thy faith may become effectual by the acknowledging of every good thing which is in you in Christ Jesus" (Philemon 1:6).

We must begin to acknowledge what we have in Christ and allow that to become our reality.

"I am come that they might have life, and that they might have it more abundantly" (John 10:10).

CHAPTER 3

Intimacy With God

While we cannot find an account of healing from Scripture through intimacy with God, the principle cannot be denied.

Moses was a man that spent time face-to-face with God (Exodus 33:11). We also have an account that Moses spent forty days and forty nights on the mount with God, at least twice (Exodus 24:18 & Exodus 34:28).

At one hundred and twenty years, it was said of Moses, "*And Moses was an hundred and twenty years old when he died: his eye was not dim, nor his natural force abated*" (Deuteronomy 34:7).

Could this be a coincidence?

Not at all, the presence of God had saturated Moses' body, and sickness could not stay there.

This is what we can call walking in health.

At one hundred and twenty years old, Moses climbed a mountain (Deuteronomy 34:1). Of course, he had to be very strong and healthy to do that, especially at that age.

CHAPTER 4

By The Word of God

God's Word is living and powerful, and sharper than any two-edged sword. God's Word is life.

We have to know that Jesus Christ, the Son of the living God, is "The Word of God".

"*And I saw heaven opened, and behold a white horse; and he that sat upon him was called Faithful and True, and in righteousness he doth judge and make war. His eyes were as a flame of fire, and on his head were many crowns; and he had a name written, that no man knew, but he himself. And he was clothed with a vesture dipped in blood:* **and his name is called The Word of God**" (Revelation 19:11-13).

"*In the beginning was the Word, and the Word was with God, and the Word was God*" (John 1:1).

We are also told that God's Word is life to those that find them and health to all their flesh

"*My son, attend to my words; incline thine ear unto my sayings. Let them not depart from thine eyes; keep them in the midst of thine heart.* **For they are life unto those** *that find them, and health to all their flesh*" (Proverbs 4:20-22).

How do we find God's Word?

Finding is an active thing. God's Word becomes life to us when we focus and meditate on it.

God's Word will heal us.

"*He sent his word, and healed them, and delivered them from their destructions*" (Psalm 107:20).

CHAPTER 5

In The Place of Worship

The presence of God is bound to affect a person's body. The Scripture says in Psalm 22:3: *"But thou art holy, O thou that inhabitest the praises of Israel"*.

The manifest presence of God will cause certain things to give way.

CHAPTER 6

By The Gifts of The Spirit

Gifts of healing and the working of miracles are one of the gifts of the Spirit.

"Now there are diversities of gifts, but the same Spirit. And there are differences of administrations, but the same Lord. And there are diversities of operations, but it is the same God which worketh all in all. But the manifestation of the Spirit is given to every man to profit withal. For to one is given by the Spirit the word of wisdom; to another the word of knowledge by the same Spirit; To another faith by the same Spirit; **to another the gifts of healing by the same Spirit;** **To another the working of miracles;** *to another prophecy; to another discerning of spirits; to another divers kinds of tongues; to another the interpretation of tongues: But all these worketh that one and the selfsame Spirit, dividing to every man severally as he will "*(1 Corinthians 12:4-10).

We can see that the gifts of healing and the working of miracles are by the Spirit. We cannot limit the working of miracles to only healing, but we will focus on the subject of healing alone in this book.

This is where we see all sorts of miracles take place when this gift is in operation.

In the life of Jesus Christ, we see both miracles (John 6:2; John 11:24) and healings (Matthew 4:24; Matthew 12:15).

In the life of the disciples in the early church, we also see miracles (Acts 6:8; Acts 8:6).

The Lord has also graced some members of the body with the gifts of miracles.

Now ye are the body of Christ, and members in particular. **And God hath set some in the church,** *first apostles, secondarily prophets, thirdly teachers,* **after that miracles, then gifts of healings**, *helps, governments, diversities of tongues* (1 Corinthians 12:27-28).

When these gifts are in operation or a person set in a church has been graced with gifts, healings and miracles occur.

CHAPTER 7

By Divine Intervention (Angels)

This is not a topic that is often mentioned. The Lord can send an angel to intervene in certain situations, and only Him can authorise their interventions.

The Scripture says, *"But to which of the angels said he at any time, Sit on my right hand, until I make thine enemies thy footstool? Are they not all ministering spirits, sent **forth to minister for them who shall be heirs of salvation**?"* (Hebrews 1:13-14).

Here, the Bible mentioned that angels are sent to minister for them who shall be heirs of salvation. That ministration can include healing.

We see in the gospels where an angel came to stir the water, and whosoever got in first was healed of whatever ailment he had.

*"After this there was a feast of the Jews; and Jesus went up to Jerusalem. Now there is at Jerusalem by the sheep market a pool, which is called in the Hebrew tongue Bethesda, having five porches. In these lay a great multitude of impotent folk, of blind, halt, withered, waiting for the moving of the water. **For an angel went down at a certain season into the pool, and troubled the water: whosoever then first after the troubling of the water stepped in was made whole of whatsoever disease he had** "*(John 5:1-4).

CHAPTER 8

By Knowing the Truth

The scriptures tell us that knowing the truth will make us free.

"Then said Jesus to those Jews which believed on him, If ye continue in my word, then are ye my disciples indeed; And ye shall know the truth, and the truth shall make you free" (John 8:31-32).

The scriptures also tell us that *"by knowledge the righteous shall be delivered"* (Proverbs 11:9).

So, what is the truth that sets us free when it comes to healing?

- Knowing that Jesus Christ has come that we may have life and have it abundantly and that it is the thief that has come to kill, steal, and destroy (John 10:10).

- Jesus Christ bore our pains and sicknesses on the cross:

"Surely he hath borne our griefs, and carried our sorrows: yet we did esteem him stricken, smitten of God, and afflicted. But he was wounded for our transgres-

sions, he was bruised for our iniquities: the chastise-ment of our peace was upon him; and with his stripes we are healed" (Isaiah 53:4-5).

-    Knowing that God wants us healed and walking in health:

"*Beloved, I wish above all things that thou mayest prosper and be in health, even as thy soul prospereth*" (3 John 2).

CHAPTER 9

By Taking Natural Remedies

In the scriptures, Paul wrote to Timothy to take wine that would help him.

"Drink no longer water, but use a little wine for thy stomach's sake and thine often infirmities" (1 Timothy 5:23).

We also have an account in the Old Testament of Hezekiah asking the Lord to heal him. The Lord gave Isaiah a message for Hezekiah, telling Hezekiah that he would be healed.

*"Turn again, and tell Hezekiah the captain of my people, Thus saith the Lord, the God of David thy father, I have heard thy prayer, I have seen thy tears: behold, I will heal thee: on the third day thou shalt go up unto the house of the Lord. And I will add unto thy days fifteen years; and I will deliver thee and this city out of the hand of the king of Assyria; and I will defend this city for mine own sake, and for my servant David's sake. **And Isaiah said, Take a lump of figs. And they took and laid it on the boil, and he recovered**"* (2 Kings 20:5-7).

We can see from the above that Hezekiah was instructed to take a lump of figs and put it on the boil,
and he recovered.

CHAPTER 10

The Prayer of Faith

In the Book of James, the scriptures tell us to call the elders of the Church when a person is sick to ask for prayer.

It is quite important that the elders believe that God is still in the healing business. This is so that they can pray in line with God's will.

"*Is any sick among you? let him call for the elders of the church; and let them pray over him, anointing him with oil in the name of the Lord: **And the prayer of faith shall save the sick**, and the Lord shall raise him up; and if he have committed sins, they shall be forgiven him*" (James 5:14-15).

Here, Scripture is very clear that the prayer of faith will save the sick.

In the Book of James, we find another scripture based on the prayer of faith. While this scripture refers to wisdom, the prayer of faith can be seen.

"*If any of you lack wisdom, let him ask of God, that giveth to all men liberally, and upbraideth not; and it shall be given him. **But let him ask in faith**, nothing* *wavering. For he that wavereth is like a wave of the sea driven with the wind and tossed, For let not that man think that he shall receive any thing of the Lord. A double minded man is unstable in all his ways"*. (James 1:5-8). The above verses give us the definition of the prayer of faith.

CHAPTER 11

Confessing Our Faults/
Praying for One Another

Why would the scriptures tell us to confess our faults one to another that we may be healed?

"Confess your faults one to another, and pray one for another, that ye may be healed. The effectual fervent prayer of a righteous man availeth much" (James 5:16).

We know that God forgives sin (1 John 1:9), and we also forgive others as the Bible clarifies that we have to forgive others.

"And be ye kind one to another, tenderhearted, forgiving one another, even as God for Christ's sake hath forgiven you" (Ephesians 4: 32).

We are told to confess our faults, i.e., our shortcomings, one to another. So, what does that mean?

I don't claim to have a full revelation of what this verse means; however, considering other verses in the Bible, it simply means that how we treat others can affect us.

Now, let us look at this verse:

"*Likewise, ye husbands, dwell with them according to knowledge, giving honour unto the wife, as unto the weaker vessel, and as* being heirs together of the grace of life; **that your prayers be not hindered"** (1 Peter 3:7).

If a husband's prayers can be hindered because of how he treats his wife, will the prayers of others not be impeded if they treat others wrongly?

The simple remedy would be to confess that fault to the person, talk it over, repent, apologise where needed, and keep prayer effective.

Following confessing our faults to one another, we are meant to pray for one another that we may be healed.

Has the Lord been prompting you to call someone and apologise to them? There could be a reason.

If a husband's prayers could be hindered for not treating his wife right, the way we treat each other is crucial.

The remedy to make a change is simple; it's simply asking the person for forgiveness and then praying for one another.

CHAPTER 12

By the Laying on of Hands

The doctrine of laying on of hands is a foundational truth in Christianity.

*"Therefore leaving the principles of the doctrine of Christ, let us go on unto perfection; not laying again the foundation of repentance from dead works, and of faith toward God, Of the doctrine of baptisms, **and of laying on of hands**, and of resurrection of the dead, and of eternal judgment"* (Hebrews 6: 1-2).

Laying on of hands is one of the principles of the doctrine of Christ.

Believers are told to lay hands on the sick, and they shall recover:

*"And these signs shall follow them that believe; In my name shall they cast out devils; they shall speak with new tongues; they shall take up serpents; and if they drink any deadly thing, it shall not hurt them; **they shall lay hands on the sick, and they shall recover**"* (Mark 16:16-18).

During the earthly ministry of our Lord Jesus Christ, He laid hands on the sick:

"*Now when the sun was setting, all they that had any sick with divers diseases brought them unto him;* **and he laid his hands on every one of them, and healed them**" (Luke 4:40).

The Apostles' hands also brought signs and wonders:

"**And by the hands** *of the apostles were many signs and wonders wrought among the people; (and they were all with one accord in Solomon's porch*" (Acts 5:12).

CHAPTER 13

By a Point of Contact

Have you heard of people praying over hand-kerchiefs and requesting them to be laid on a sick person?

This is another method found from Scripture that people received their healing.

"And God wrought special miracles by the hands of Paul: So that from his body were brought unto the sick handkerchiefs or aprons, and the diseases departed from them, and the evil spirits went out of them" (Acts 19:11-12).

This is how the woman with the issue of blood in the gospels received her healing:

"And a certain woman, which had an issue of blood twelve years, And had suffered many things of many physicians, and had spent all that she had, and was nothing bettered, but rather grew worse, when she had heard of Jesus, came in the press behind, and touched his garment. **For she said, If I may touch but his clothes, I shall be whole. And straightway the fountain of her blood was dried up; and she felt in her body that**

she was healed of that plague. And Jesus, immediately knowing in himself that virtue had gone out of him, turned him about in the press, and said, Who touched my clothes? And his disciples said unto him, Thou seest the multitude thronging thee, and sayest thou, Who touched me? And he looked round about to see her that had done this all the truth. And he said unto her, **Daughter, thy faith hath made thee** *whole; go in peace, and be whole of thy plague"* (Mark 5:31-34).

This woman had faith that if she only touched Jesus' garments, she would be healed, and she was. As a result, this woman initiated her own healing.

The anointed shadow of Peter also healed the sick.

"And by the hands of the apostles were many signs and wonders wrought among the people; (and they were all with one accord in Solomon's porch. And of the rest durst no man join himself to them: but the people magnified them. And believers were the more added to the Lord, multitudes both of men and women.) **Insomuch that they brought forth the sick into the streets, and laid them on beds and couches, that at the least the shadow of Peter passing by might overshadow some of them.** *There came also a multitude out of the cities round about unto Jerusalem, bringing sick folks, and them which were vexed with unclean spirits:* **and they were healed every one"** (Acts 5:12-16).

CHAPTER 14

Dealing With Issues in the Soul

How we think (including our mindsets) can affect our health.

The Bible says, "...as a man thinks in his heart so is he" (Proverbs 23:7).

This is one reason we are instructed to renew our minds (Romans 12:2).

There is a connection between the state of our souls and our health.

"Beloved, I wish above all things that thou mayest prosper and be in health, even as thy soul prospereth" (3 John 2).

It simply means the right adjustments in a person will positively affect their health.

Now, let's look at some scriptures that speak for themselves:

"A sound heart is the life of the flesh: but envy the rottenness of the bones" (Proverbs 14:30).

"A merry heart doeth good like a medicine: but a broken spirit drieth the bones "(Proverbs 17:22).

CHAPTER 15

Acting on Your Faith

W hile this has been implied in some of the earlier examples, it is good practice to highlight it. This is because, in many instances of healing, Jesus said, "Thy faith has made thee whole" (Mark 5:34 and Mark 10:52). We can also see the phrase "when Jesus saw their faith" (Mark 2:5), which resulted in a person getting healed.

The phrase "thy faith hath made thee whole" indicates that the individual initiated the healing.

Let us have a further look:

"*And a certain woman, which had an issue of blood twelve years, And had suffered many things of many physicians, and had spent all that she had, and was nothing bettered, but rather grew worse,* **When she had heard of Jesus**, *came in the press behind, and touched his garment.* **For she said, If I may touch but his clothes, I shall be whole**. *And straightway the fountain of her blood was dried up; and she felt in her body that she was healed of that plague. And Jesus, immediately knowing in himself that virtue had gone out of him,* *turned him about in the press, and said, Who touched my clothes? And his disciples said unto him, Thou seest the multitude thronging thee, and sayest thou, Who touched me? And he looked round about to see her that had done this thing. But the woman fearing and trembling, knowing what was done in her, came and fell down before him, and told him all the truth. And he said unto her, Daughter, thy faith hath made thee whole; go in peace, and be whole of thy plague"* (Mark 5:25-34).

From the above, we see the following:

- This woman heard of Jesus.
- She said that if she could just touch His garment, she would be made whole.
- She acted on what she believed and was made whole.

"And they came to Jericho: and as he went out of Jericho with his disciples and a great number of people, blind Bartimaeus, the son of Timaeus, sat by the highway side begging. **And when he heard that it was Jesus of Nazareth, he began to cry out,** *and say, Jesus, thou son of David, have mercy on me.* **And many charged him that he** *should hold his peace:* **but he cried the more a great deal, Thou son of David, have mercy on me.** *And Jesus stood still, and commanded him to be called. And they call the blind man, saying unto him, Be of good comfort, rise; he calleth thee. And he, casting away his garment, rose, and came to Jesus. And Jesus answered and said unto him, What wilt thou that I should do*

*unto thee? The blind man said unto him, Lord, that I might receive my sight. **And Jesus said unto him, Go thy way; thy faith hath** made thee whole. And immediately he received his sight, and followed Jesus in the way"* (Mark 10: 46-52).

From this scripture, we see the following:

- Blind Bartimaeus, the son of Timaeus, heard that Jesus was passing by.
- He then began to cry, *thou Son of David, have mercy on me.*
- People tried to stop him from crying out.
- He did not allow the response of others to stop him from crying out.
- His persistence got Jesus' attention.
- He received his sight immediately.

Let us look at another account.

"And straightway many were gathered together, insomuch that there was no room to receive them, no, not so much as about the door: and he preached the word unto them. And they come unto him, bringing one sick of the palsy, which was borne of four. And when they could not come nigh unto him for the press, they uncovered the roof where he was: and when they had broken it up, they let down the bed wherein the sick of the palsy lay. When Jesus saw their faith, he said unto the sick of the palsy, Son, thy sins be forgiven thee. But there was certain of the scribes sitting there, and reasoning in their hearts, Why doth this man thus speak blasphemies? who can forgive sins but God only? And immediately when Jesus perceived in his spirit that they so reasoned

within themselves, he said unto them, Why reason ye these things in your hearts? Whether is it easier to say to the sick of the palsy, Thy sins be forgiven thee; or to say, Arise, and take up thy bed, and walk? But that ye may know that the Son of man hath power on earth to forgive sins, (he saith to the sick of the palsy,) I say unto thee, **Arise, and take up thy bed, and go thy way into thine house. And immediately he arose, took up the bed, and went forth before them all; insomuch that they were all amazed, and glorified God, saying, We never saw it on this fashion**" (Mark 2:2-12).

From the above verses of Scripture, we see the following:

- Four people brought in a man and decided to uncover the roof and break it up to get the man to Jesus.
- Jesus saw their faith, i.e., their persistence.
- Their faith here was, whatever it takes, we must get our friend to Jesus even if it means breaking the roof.
- This resulted in the man receiving his healing.

So, we can see from the above few examples of what it means to act on your faith. They all acted on what they believed. To the woman with the issue of blood, this meant her touching Jesus's garment; to blind Bartimaeus, the son of Timaeus, it meant him shouting and crying even louder when others told him to keep quiet. And to those that wanted to help the sick man, nothing was going to stop them from getting to Jesus. In this case, it took breaking the roof.

While this book talks about healing, acting on our faith applies to many areas of life.

CHAPTER 16

The Power of the Tongue

What we say can affect our health. Therefore, we must be cautious with our words.

"Death and life are in the power of the tongue: and they that love it shall eat the fruit thereof. Death and life are in the power of the tongue: and they that love it shall eat the fruit thereof" (Proverbs 18:21).

*"There is that speaketh like the piercings of a sword: but the tongue of the wise is **health**"* (Proverbs 12:18).

*"Pleasant words are as an honeycomb, sweet to the soul, **and health to the bones**"* (Proverbs 16:24).

These scriptures speak for themselves.

I know that we have talked about speaking to the situation, but this section looks at the continuous function of the tongue—things that we say on a daily basis.

The scriptures are clear that we need to watch what we say.

CHAPTER 17

Casting Our Cares Upon the Lord

L earning to cast our cares upon the Lord is a great contribution to walking in health. It is God's peace that keeps our hearts and minds through Christ Jesus.

*"Be careful for nothing; but in every thing by prayer and supplication with thanksgiving let your requests be made known unto God. **And the peace of God,** which passeth all understanding, **shall keep your hearts and minds through Christ Jesus**"* (Philippians 4:6-7).

This scripture tells us what we need to do with our cares. It includes everything. Nothing is too small for the Lord.

The Bible says, "Be careful for nothing". Nothing means nothing. We must learn to cast all our cares upon the Lord.

"Thou wilt keep him in perfect peace, whose mind is stayed on thee: because he trusteth in thee" (Isaiah 26:3).

CHAPTER 18

The Fear of The Lord

Not a popular topic today; however, the scriptures are clear and remain the truth that endures to all generations (Psalm 100:5).

The fear of the Lord will cause us to walk uprightly, which will impact our health. There are certain things that we will not do with our bodies when we walk in the fear of the Lord. The Bible tells us to glorify God in our bodies, which are God's (1 Corinthians 6:20).

"Be not wise in thine own eyes: fear the Lord, and depart from evil. **It shall be health to thy navel, and marrow to thy bones"** (Proverbs 3:7-8).

CHAPTER 19

Cure for Unbelief

The book will not be complete without looking at the cure for unbelief.

Faith is vital in our walk with the Lord. The good news is that we have all been given the measure of faith (Romans 12:3).

As Christians, we are instructed to walk by faith and not by sight (2 Corinthians 5:7).

So, what is faith?

In simple terms, faith is acting on what you believe.

The Book of Hebrews gives us a definition of faith: *"Now faith is the substance of things hoped for, the evidence of things not seen"* (Hebrews 11:1).

We see the Lord rebuke His disciples for little faith (Matthew 8:26) and unbelief (Matthew 17:20).

So, what is the cure for unbelief? One cure for unbelief is knowing the love of the Father.

God loves us, and God is love (1 John 4:7). Faith works better by acknowledging and knowing the love of the Father.

For faith works by love (Galatians 5:6).

Another cure for unbelief is knowing the integrity of God's Word.

"For ever, O Lord, thy word is settled in heaven" (Psalm 119:89).

"For thou hast magnified thy word above all thy name" (Psalm 138:2).

CONCLUSION

God wants us in sound and good health, so be encouraged.

This book is just a snapshot of various ways healing can be received. I would recommend that you explore them through different ministries that are already ministering healing.

In most cases, many ministries will minister healing through some of the selected ways stated in this book. A good example is a ministry that operates with the working of miracles. You will find many notable miracles taking place under such a ministry.

The good news is that there are various other ways to receive healing.

If you attend a healing meeting and your case is not called out, that is not the end.

Perhaps after attending so many healing services, it might be an idea to sit down with God's Word, find out what it says, and meditate on the truth.

It is the truth that makes us free.

The Holy Spirit will guide us into all truth, and the truth is, "God wants us well".

So, if you are being led to do something that is not

the norm within your environment of influence, don't ignore it.

The Lord might be saying, "Change your diet". On the other hand, you might sense all you need to do is thank the Lord that it is done, or the Lord may be nudging us to be mindful of our words. Remember, it is the Holy Spirit that guides us into all truth.

Whatever the Lord says we should do, or you sense to do, just do it.

SALVATION PRAYER

F ather God, l come to you in Jesus' name. I admit that I am a sinner, and l now receive the sacrifice that Jesus Christ paid for me.

I confess with my mouth the Lord Jesus, and l believe in my heart that God raised Him from the dead.

I now declare that Jesus Christ is my Lord and Saviour.

Thank you, Father, for saving me in Jesus' name.

I am now your child. Amen.

If you've said this prayer for the first time, send an email to bisiwriter@outlook.com. Start reading your Bible and ask the Lord to guide you to a good church.

ABOUT THE AUTHOR

Bisi Oladipupo has been a Christian for many years and lives in the United Kingdom with her family.

Bisi attended a few Bible colleges and obtained a Biblical Studies diploma from a UK Bible college.

She is a teacher of God's Word, coordinates Bible studies, and has a YouTube channel at https://www.youtube.com/c/BisiOladipupo123.

She writes regularly, and her website is www.inspiredwords.org

You can contact Bisi by email at bisiwriter@outlook.com.

QR Code for Bisi's Linktree:

OTHER BOOKS BY BISI

The Twelve Apostles of Jesus Christ: Lessons We Can Learn

THE LORD'S CUP IN COMMUNION: The Significance of taking the Lord's Supper

Printed in Great Britain
by Amazon